MIAMI

THE CITY AT A GL

MW00860723

South Pointe Park
Cruise ships head to sea past this 2009 park landscaped by Hargreaves Associates. Watch the action over a steak at Smith & Wollensky (1 Washington Avenue, T 305 673 2800).

Four Seasons
In 2003, this 240m hotel/condo became Florida's tallest building. It was supplanted in 2018 by the nearby Panorama Tower, which rises 252m but is otherwise uninspiring, also located on Miami's answer to Wall Street.
1435 Brickell Avenue

Portofino Tower
The brash turquoise-orange 1990s skyscraper is impossible to miss. Its lucky residents have superb views, and don't have to look at it.
See p012

Icon Brickell
These apartment towers on the river are a symbol of the excesses of the mid-2000s real-estate boom – the build cost more than $1bn.
See p013

MacArthur Causeway
Any movie about the city usually involves an overhead of this palm-tree-lined causeway, which connects the mainland to 5th Street.

One Thousand Museum
Zaha Hadid was finishing off these curvaceous 62 floors when she passed away here in 2016. It is not a museum at all, just another condo, but does point the way to PAMM (see p034).
1000 Biscayne Boulevard

Star Island
Home to the super-rich and Miami royalty Gloria Esteban, Don Johnson and P Diddy, whose pool alone can hold 200 people.

INTRODUCTION
THE CHANGING FACE OF THE URBAN SCENE

The South Beach dream was hatched 30 years ago when model agencies and photographers discovered its cheap art deco hotels and ocean views. Many of those who created the scene have left, died or gone to prison – Miami has long had a reputation as a sunny hideout for shady people. But then, as novelist Carl Hiaasen wrote: 'Just because a place is shallow, corrupt and infested with phonies doesn't mean it's dull.' And it's true that you'll see hard bodies roller-blading in bikinis, muscle boys pumping iron, palm trees dropping coconuts, imported sand, imported chests, convertibles blasting hip hop and *everyone* on iPhones, trawling photos of last night's párty.

Today, Miami is also a halfway house for fabulously wealthy Latinos, Russians and Europeans fleeing troubled economies, who have stretched oceanside development north to Surfside and Sunny Isles to avoid the weekend ruckus. This cash, coupled with the Art Basel effect, which has injected genuine gravitas and self-worth, has led to a raft of cultural additions, from high-profile museums to independent galleries, and turned the metropolis into an emerging architectural wonderland, tempting Herzog & de Meuron, Frank Gehry, Bjarke Ingels and Nicolas Grimshaw to spend time in the sun. A word of advice: much of the evolution is on the mainland. So cross the bay to Wynwood, Museum Park, Little River and the slice of restored MiMo lining Biscayne Boulevard. Frivolous Miami has matured into a sophisticated city unimaginable a decade ago.

ESSENTIAL INFO
FACTS, FIGURES AND USEFUL ADDRESSES

TOURIST OFFICE
Greater Miami Visitors Bureau
701 Brickell Avenue
T 305 539 3000
www.miamiandbeaches.com

TRANSPORT
Airport transfer to city centre
Metrorail trains depart every 30 minutes
(15 at weekends) from 5am to midnight to
Brickell. The journey takes half an hour
Public transport
The elevated Metromover and Metrorail
services run from 5am to midnight
T 305 891 3131
www.miamidade.gov/transit
Car hire
Avis
T 305 538 4441
Taxis
Yellow Cabs
T 305 897 3333
There are no taxi ranks and hailing a cab
away from South Beach can be difficult

EMERGENCY SERVICES
Emergencies
T 911
US Coast Guard
T 305 535 4472
24-hour pharmacy
Walgreens
1011 Alton Road
T 305 424 1145

CONSULATE
British Consulate
Brickell Bay Office Tower
1001 Brickell Bay Drive
T 305 400 6400
www.gov.uk/world/organisations/
british-consulate-general-miami

POSTAL SERVICES
Post office
1300 Washington Avenue
T 305 672 2447
Shipping
UPS
T 305 538 5076

BOOKS
Back to Blood by Tom Wolfe
(Little, Brown)
Miami Architecture by Allan T Shulman,
Randall C Robinson Jr and James F
Donnelly (University Press of Florida)
Tourist Season by Carl Hiaasen
(Pan Macmillan)

WEBSITES
Art/Design
www.miamidesigndistrict.net
www.wynwoodmiami.com
Newspaper
www.miamiherald.com

EVENTS
Art Basel Miami Beach
www.artbaselmiamibeach.com
Design Miami
www.designmiami.com

COST OF LIVING
**Taxi from Miami International Airport
to South Beach**
$40
Cappuccino
$4
Packet of cigarettes
$7.25
Daily newspaper
$2
Bottle of champagne
$95

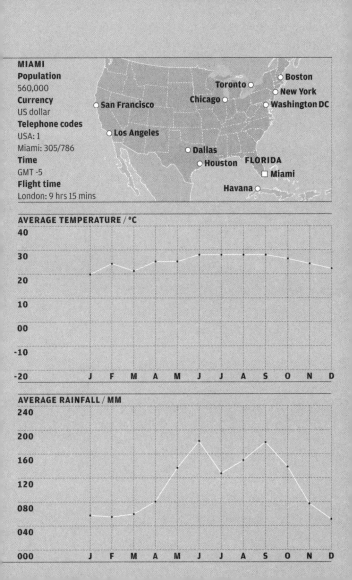

MIAMI
Population
560,000
Currency
US dollar
Telephone codes
USA: 1
Miami: 305/786
Time
GMT -5
Flight time
London: 9 hrs 15 mins

Toronto
Boston
New York
Chicago
Washington DC
San Francisco
Los Angeles
Dallas
Houston
FLORIDA
Miami
Havana

AVERAGE TEMPERATURE / °C

40
30
20
10
00
-10
-20

J F M A M J J A S O N D

AVERAGE RAINFALL / MM

240
200
160
120
080
040
000

J F M A M J J A S O N D

NEIGHBOURHOODS
THE AREAS YOU NEED TO KNOW AND WHY

To help you navigate the city, we've chosen the most interesting districts (see below and the map inside the back cover) and colour-coded our featured venues, according to their location; those venues that are outside these areas are not coloured.

CORAL GABLES/COCONUT GROVE
From its beginnings in the 1920s, Coral Gables was constructed predominantly in the Mediterranean revival style — Merrick House (907 Coral Way, T 305 460 5361) is a fine example. Among its listed buildings is the Biltmore Hotel (1200 Anastasia Avenue, T 855 311 6903), a magnificent 1926 pile. Coconut Grove's bohemian vibe, and leafy residential charm, has been shaken up by contemporary statements by BIG and OMA.

SOUTH BEACH
The art deco district stretches between 5th Street and Lincoln Road. Ocean Drive was the heart of SoBe's 1990s rebirth, but the action moved north as Collins Avenue became hot. The Standard (see p035) and the Mondrian hotels have moved in to the residential enclave facing Biscayne Bay, the Bass (see p036) has been reborn, and 1111 Lincoln Road (see p010) and the New World Center (see p038) were the first architectural projects here in decades.

MIMO DISTRICT
Biscayne Boulevard was the prime tourist route into Miami before the interstate was built, and strung along it are the remaining examples of the MiMo movement, from gas stations to signage and motels, such as the Vagabond (see p030). The area also boasts various gems by influential local architects, including Wahl Snyder's former residence (530 Grand Concourse) and Arquitectonica's first work, Pink House (9325 N Bay Road).

DESIGN DISTRICT
The vision of art collector Craig Robins, the Design District is getting bigger and bolder. High-profile public installations and global fashion labels jostle to get one over their neighbours with high-concept stores, while the shiny ICA (see p074) vies for attention with the city's most outlandish garage (see p068). There's a foodie flourish too, thanks to celebrity gourmet collaborations such as Swan (90 NE 39th Street, T 305 704 0994).

DOWNTOWN/WYNWOOD
A lively cultural quarter has consolidated as PAMM (see p034) has given the area's rejuvenation real impetus. The Downtown financial centre is home to a multiplying cluster of (often bland) towers of offices, banks, hotels and condos (see p013). The Wynwood warehouses have been turned into bustling bars, clubs and cafés, drawing ever greater numbers to some impressive private galleries (see p032) and forcing the hipsters out to Little River (see p067).

MIAMI BEACH
There is only limited beachfront here, so old stamping grounds are constantly being rediscovered. The lynchpins of the 1950s boom — Morris Lapidus' Fontainebleau (see p081) and Eden Roc (4525 Collins Avenue, T 305 531 0000) — have now been joined by the Faena District (see p018) and rebirth of The Surf Club (see p022). To the north are the Bal Harbour Shops (see p088) retail hub and the MiMo of Bay Harbor Islands.

LANDMARKS

THE SHAPE OF THE CITY SKYLINE

This is one of the youngest urban areas in the USA – Miami was founded only in 1896. The outlying barrier island of Miami Beach, much of it reclaimed land, was incorporated in 1915, connected by a series of causeways. Making up the remainder of the metropolis is Coral Gables, which was one of the first planned communities in the States and is known for its Mediterranean revival architecture.

In the past 20 years, the city has become the economic gateway to Latin America, resulting in a line of towers on Biscayne Bay that have formed a characterless sea wall. Standouts are the 240m Four Seasons (see p016) and KPF's Brickell Arch (1395 Brickell Avenue). Some cultural depth has arrived with PAMM (see p034) and Cesar Pelli's Adrienne Arsht Center (1300 Biscayne Boulevard, T 305 949 6722), while commercial expansion continues unfettered. Brickell City Centre spans five blocks of retail, offices and hotel (see p025), and the proposed, long delayed Skyrise (Bayside Marketplace) is a 302m-tall open-sided viewing deck that resembles a hair clip.

At least developers have recognised the value a Pritzker Prize tag can add, and Zaha Hadid's One Thousand Museum (1000 Biscayne Boulevard), Renzo Piano's Eighty Seven Park (8701 Collins Avenue) and Jean Nouvel's Monad Terrace (1300 Monad Terrace) do have personality. And talented locals such as Rene Gonzalez (see p082) instil a sense of place to these rarely occupied, mega-money condos. *For full addresses, see Resources.*

1111 Lincoln Road

You might wonder what the deal is with
Miami Beach and parking garages. It's all
about geology. It doesn't make sense to dig
underground when water gushes out of the
drains at high tide. So they went up instead.
But it was not until Herzog & de Meuron's
commission for 1111 Lincoln Road in 2008
that anyone had thought to design them
or add to their primary purpose. Here, at
ground level, retail and eateries surround
a plaza; Alchemist has a store (see p094)
on level five; there's art under the stairs;
and rooftop restaurant Juvia (see p060)
is accessed via the Suntrust building. The
client tacked a penthouse with gardens by
Raymond Jungles above the striking 2010
concrete structure. It was sold for $283m in
2017, sparking a frenzy as developers try to
replicate its mixed-use formula (see p068).
www.1111lincolnrd.com

Portofino Tower

In the 1980s, south of 5th Street, or SoFi, was a no-man's-land with an oil refinery, a meat-packing plant, storage tanks, derelict open space and the venerable fish palace Joe's Stone Crab (T 305 673 0365), which is still going strong. But German developer Thomas Kramer saw something else: views of Downtown and of cruise ships heading out to sea, in an enclave not constrained by the height limits of the art deco district.

His 147.5m condominium tower opened in 1997, replete with brightly coloured curves, abutments, wings and an Italianate crown. Architects Sieger Suarez would later ditch this bold look and produce many insipid high-rises. A number now crowd around Portofino, as does Rene Gonzalez's stylish Glass (see p082), yet it still holds its own as an outsider's fantasy of beach living.
300 S Pointe Drive

Icon Brickell

This trio of towers, resembling radiators, houses 1,648 apartments and the W hotel (T 305 503 4400), which boasts the city's most elevated pool, on the 50th floor. The design is by Arquitectonica but you might not realise it – in Miami, buildings become known more for their interiors, and hence Icon Brickell is recognised as the work of Philippe Starck. To be fair, the Frenchman has made his mark on the exterior – with a collection of 6.7m columns in the shape of creepy Easter Island-style heads. The pillars are used throughout, as are other Starckisms, such as the giant chessboard on the 15th-floor terrace. The complex is also a symbolic landmark – following the property market collapse, the developer handed two of the towers back to HSBC in 2010 to avoid defaulting on its loans. *475 Brickell Avenue, www.iconbrickell.com*

Atlantis

Arquitectonica's 1982 Atlantis is arguably the city's most recognisable landmark, at least for anyone who can remember the TV series *Miami Vice*. Each episode began with a shot of its glass facade, showing the four-and-a-half-storey cut-out featuring a red spiral staircase, a palm tree and a pale-blue jacuzzi, as well as the striking triangle perched on the roof. This 20-storey block with 96 condos offered an exotic, urban lifestyle and made its architects famous. It was built during the cocaine boom, when so much drug money was stuffed into the banks that it impacted the skyline – they loaned to anyone wanting to develop along Brickell. Unfortunately, several high-rises and a lot of vegetation now block the view, so you'll need to look that little bit harder or take to the sidewalk – Miami does have them – to check out this postmodern icon.
2025 Brickell Avenue

HOTELS

WHERE TO STAY AND WHICH ROOMS TO BOOK

The SoBe scene starts on Ocean Drive with the revamped The Betsy (see po28), and moves on to Collins Avenue, which has direct sand access, with the Delano (see po29), the hip Kimpton Surfcomber (No 1717, T 305 532 7715), the Nautilus (see po24), the W (see po26) and chic Ibiza-style 1 Hotel (No 2341, T 305 604 1000). Back from the sea, art deco refurb The Plymouth (336 21st Street, T 305 602 5000) on Collins Square has a Saint-Tropez vibe. While the sceney hotels lack Claridge's-style service, there will be a vibey bar, a pool party, hip stores and branded restaurants. To the north, Faena's fantasy playground (see po18) has joined pioneer Soho Beach House (opposite), happening Freehand (2727 Indian Creek Drive, T 305 531 2727), Edition (see po21) and the Martin Brudnizki-designed The Confidante (No 4041, T 305 424 1234) in a mid-beach cluster.

Downtown's hotels are more business-oriented, including the Four Seasons (1435 Brickell Avenue, T 305 358 3535) and the swish Mandarin Oriental (500 Brickell Key Drive, T 305 913 8288). The design properties found here, such as East (see po25), the Kimpton Epic (270 Biscayne Boulevard, T 305 424 5226) and the W (see po13), are better value than those on the ocean. Elsewhere, The Vagabond (see po30) is now a MiMo anchor, and the Ciprianis have woken up sleepy Coconut Grove with a nautical version of their Mr C (2988 McFarlane Road, T 866 786 4173) concept, launched in 2019. *For full addresses and room rates, see Resources.*

Soho Beach House

The buzzy hospitality-chic Soho House hallmarks are all in place at this outpost, which dropped anchor in 2010 inside Roy France's converted 1941 art deco Sovereign Hotel and Allan Shulman's new 16-storey tower. The signature Cowshed spa, which is furnished with vintage barbers' chairs, Cecconi's (above, T 786 507 7902), a lively Venetian-style brasserie, and two pools are open to non-guests. The Cuban-inspired interiors exude a welcoming lived-in feel, and mix salvaged timber with church tiles, distressed leather armchairs, raw concrete beams and one-off furniture pieces, while swathes of light blues inject a breezy cool. A few Beachside rooms have terraces and bathtubs with ocean views; *Mad Men*-esque wet bars cap the hedonistic experience. *4385 Collins Avenue, T 786 507 7900, www.sohobeachhouse.com*

Faena

A monumental clash with Philippe Starck over the original BA incarnation prompted Argentine developer Alan Faena to change tack here, hiring filmmaker Baz Luhrmann to 'direct' his blockbuster inside the former Saxony Hotel, a modernist gem from 1948. It opened in 2015 with an Art Basel roller disco, Damien Hirst's gold mammoth in the garden and unicorn in pan-Asian restaurant Pao by Paul Qui (T 786 655 5600), Juan Gatti's monumental paintings in the gilded lobby and furniture by Brad Pitt. Faena's OTT decor is pure old-school Miami. In the rooms, its trademark ruby red (Premier Oceanfront Corner Suite, above) plays off teal, darkwood and marble. There's also a steakhouse grill, a quasi-psychedelic spa, and burlesque at the womb-like theatre.
3201 Collins Avenue, T 305 534 8800, www.faena.com/miami-beach

COMO Metropolitan

You may leave here with a new favourite colour – pale pistachio. Italian designer Paola Navone has used a soothing palette in this boutique property for Singaporean chain COMO, which is known for its style and service. It is an updating of Albert Anis' 1939 hotel, with banquettes ringing giant columns in the lobby, savvy touches like the Serge Mouille five- and seven-arm wall sconces and a hydrotherapy pool on the roof (above). The 74 rooms, in particular the Ocean View Suite, are spacious for the district, and Traymore restaurant serves healthy local cuisine overseen by Miami darling Michael Schwartz. Set right on the beach, just north of the sceney hotels, the Metropolitan offers relative quiet a stroll from the New World Center (see p038).
2445 Collins Avenue, T 305 695 3600, www.comohotels.com

Edition

Every decade there's one Miami hotel that sets the standard. In 1994, Ian Schrager's Delano (see p029) kickstarted the whole South Beach scene with a seductive, lively lobby. In 2004, the ultra-luxury Setai (not Schrager) appealed to a billionaire crowd that discovered Miami through Art Basel. And, in late 2014, Edition (Schrager again) established a new level of hip. It succeeds in every way. Jean-Georges Vongerichten is in the kitchen, Steven Giles (see p089) oversees the retail and Yabu Pushelberg devised the marble lobby (above), throwing in a curveball with Maurizio Galante's 'Tato Tattoo' marble-print poufs, which confuse many a newcomer. Other playful touches are the danceclub that's actually meant for dancing, a bowling alley and a skating rink. *2901 Collins Avenue, T 786 257 4500, www.editionhotels.com/miami-beach*

Four Seasons at The Surf Club

The Surf Club, where Elizabeth Taylor and Frank Sinatra once hung out, was reborn in 2017 as the anchor of Richard Meier's complex of three glass towers, the middle of which cantilevers above and houses the contemporary wing of the Four Seasons. Interiors are by Joseph Dirand, and the 77 pitch-perfect rooms are a mellow blend of coastal tones, creamy hand-cut travertine, hardwood furnishings, brass fixtures and rattan panels – options also encompass a series of reconditioned Cabana Studios in Russell Pancoast's original 1930 premises. For groups, the Marybelle Penthouse Suite (above and opposite) has four beds and a pool. Restored features, such as the arched entrance colonnade, maintain a timeless splendour, as does Le Sirenuse (T 786 482 2280), which serves south Italian cuisine within a verdant colonial-style setting.
9011 Collins Avenue, T 305 381 3333,
www.fourseasons.com/surfside

Nautilus by Arlo

Revered Fontainebleau (see p081) architect Morris Lapidus also left his MiMo signature throughout the Nautilus when it opened in 1951, installing a porte-cochère, decorative 'stairway to nowhere', marble columns and double-height ceilings (lobby, above, with a chandelier inspired by Max Ingrand's 1954 'Dahlia' pendant). Naturally, Arquitectonica preserved these gems when it repurposed the hotel in 2015. Its 250 rooms, overseen by local designer Caroline Giraud-Sukornyk, have a vintage travel theme with photos by Sante D'Orazio and steamer trunks acting as minibars. The pretty boltholes around the seawater pool are good for disco naps. Have a sharpener at the midcentury-style bar and dine on Med fare on the Cabana Club's (T 786 483 2650) lovely wood deck. *1825 Collins Avenue, T 305 503 5700, www.arlohotels.com/nautilus-by-arlo*

East

Clad in asymmetrical balconies intended to evoke cascading water, Arquitectonica's 157m hotel tower lords it over Brickell City Centre (see p009). Designed by Clodagh, the 352 apartment-style pads (East Suite, above) feature wood floors, plush fabrics and watery canvases; Corner Kings have an in-your-face view of Downtown's high-rises. East is anchored by feng shui, a tone set in the lobby with an installation of burnished copper pipes. The architects opened up the fifth floor for an expansive pool and patio for Uruguayan *parrillada* Quinto La Huella (T 786 805 4646), Miami's top steakhouse, shaded by a cheesehole concrete screen. Mix in cocktails and thrilling panoramas at the rooftop garden bar Sugar (T 786 805 4655), and you won't even miss the beach. *788 Brickell Plaza, T 305 712 7000, www.east-miami.com*

W South Beach

When architect Costas Kondylis' W opened back in 2009 at 22nd Street, it expanded the boundaries of hip South Beach, which had ended with the Setai, inaugurated in 2004 two blocks south. In Miami, a swank property might face a tacky drugstore, or sit next to a fleabag motel. However, since construction was ramped up again in 2011, destination resorts have been launching much further up Collins (see p021). But the W, with 408 ocean-facing rooms (Extreme Wow, right), restaurants Mr Chow (T 305 695 1695) and The Dutch (T 305 938 3111), the Wall club (T 305 938 3130) and a Bliss spa (T 305 938 3123), is as exciting as ever. Designer Anna Busta has split the buzzy, sprawling Living Room lobby into intimate corners of tufted leather ottomans or slate velvet armchairs; artworks by Basquiat and Warhol are from owner Aby Rosen's stash.
2201 Collins Avenue, T 305 938 3000, www.wsouthbeach.com

The Betsy

For The Betsy's 2016 rebirth, legendary Miami architect Allan Shulman conjured a piece of alchemy to join Henry Hohauser's 1938 art deco Carlton Hotel on Collins to Lawrence Murray Dixon's 1941 Georgian-revivial colonial-style mansion facing the sea behind it. On the south side, a rooftop pool straddles the buildings above a shared courtyard; to the north they are linked via a corridor concealed within a bulbous orb.

Designers Carmelina Santoro and Diamante Pedersoli have achieved a breezy, homely feel, with walnut, oak and raffia ceilings in the deco wing (Skyline Penthouse, above). French chef Laurent Tourondel's LT Steak & Seafood (T 305 673 0044) is far superior to the tacky options on Ocean Drive, and there is a strong cultural programme too. *1440 Ocean Drive, T 305 531 6100, www.thebetsyhotel.com*

Delano

Its 1947 tower is recognisable for Robert Swartburg's soaring four-pronged crown, and interiors are as distinct for Philippe Starck's lobby shtick (Alice in Wonderland-inspired furniture, Dalí's 'Leda' chair and a translucent piano gifted by Lenny Kravitz), an integral part of the 1994 renovation that convinced P Diddy et al to venture to then-seedy SoBe. Rooms are restrained, flushed in all-white schemes that accentuate the ocean vistas, and small for the price, but common areas make up for it. The palm-tree-lined pool (above) is a playroom with underwater speakers; Agua Spa (T 305 674 6100) is a rooftop oasis; indoor/outdoor restaurant Leynia fuses an Argentine grill with Japanese touches; and The Florida Room (see p056) still draws the glitterati. *1685 Collins Avenue, T 305 672 2000, www.delano-hotel.com*

The Vagabond Hotel

Six years after he gifted Miami the Delano (see p029), architect Robert Swartburg was in a generous mood again with the 1953 Vagabond, which Avra Jain revamped into a stylish retro hotel in 2014 to anchor her visionary transformation of this stretch of Biscayne Boulevard. The property's neon sign (opposite), with its biomorphic stars, cantilevered porte-cochère and tiled pool (above), with a mermaid on the bottom, are emblematic of 1950s MiMo. There are teal couches and sputnik chandeliers, and rooms have midcentury-style furniture. The poolside cocktail bar is often lively, and the 'hood is on the up – hipsters hang out in nearby speakeasy The Anderson (T 305 757 3368). Across the road is a cheeky slice of Americana, the 1958 Coppertone sign.
7301 Biscayne Boulevard, T 305 400 8420, www.thevagabondhotelmiami.com

24 HOURS

SEE THE BEST OF THE CITY IN JUST ONE DAY

Visitors come to Miami for fun and sun, but there's plenty beyond the beach and clubs, much of it over the causeways. You will need a car, though, and ideally a driver, and note that at night in SoBe it is often cheaper to take a cab rather than fork out for valet parking. The city now prides itself as an arts hub; among the best venues, many of which are privately owned, are The Margulies Collection and de la Cruz Collection (see p076), PAMM (se p034), The Bass (see p036), the Rubell (see p066) and the ICA (see p074), a project of Craig Robins, *châtelain* of the Design District (opposite).

There are organised walks through Wynwood on the second Saturday of the month, when most of the area's 100 or so galleries, design emporia, fashion boutiques and antiques stores open until 10pm. For sustenance in this part of town, head to Kush (2003 N Miami Avenue, T 305 576 4500), for craft beer, 'alligator bites' and burgers, or MC Kitchen (see p061). In the evening, depending on your location, try Stubborn Seed (see p039), Alter (see p042) or the garden at Mandolin Aegean Bistro (4312 NE 2nd Avenue, T 305 749 9140). After dinner, the night may still be young. If you happen to be wearing sensible shoes, drop by bohemian Gramps (176 NW 24th Street, T 305 699 2669) or the tequila den behind the bathrooms at Coyo Taco (2300 NW 2nd Ave, T 305 573 8228). For those in heels, the Saxony Bar at the Faena (see p018) mixes fine cocktails.
For full addresses, see Resources.

BREAKFAST
OVERNIGHT OATS   GFV
OTL GRANOLA   GFV
SEASONAL FRUIT BOWL   GFV
AVOCADO TOAST   V
SUPER SEED BUTTER TOAST V
TORTILLA ESPAÑOLA   GF
EGG AND CHEESE SANDWICH

SANDWICHES
HAM & CHEESE
MANCHEGO & PEAR
CHICKEN SALAD
GRILLED CHEESE

SALADS
BABY GREENS & CITRUS
RED CABBAGE   GF V
KALE SALAD   GF V
MARKET GRAIN BOW   V

09.30 OTL

Out To Lunch (OTL) serves a healthy all-day menu with a host of gluten-free and vegan options, cold-pressed juices and shots and craft coffee to the figure-conscious types of the Design District. Kick off the morning with organic granola with hemp seeds and coconut; avocado toast with pickled red onions; or a breakfast burrito (scrambled egg, black beans, pepper, onion and salsa). Local firm Deft Union's interiors encourage a creative lot to linger – the Nate Lowman art and baby-blue and pink palette are as easy on the eye as the footfall. Upstairs, a gallery shows art and hosts fashion pop-ups. The retail architecture around here, if not the merchandise, is highly original: see 212box's bark-clad Christian Louboutin and Valerio Olgiati's marble palace for Celine. *160 NE 40th Street, T 786 953 7620, www.otlmia.com*

11.00 Pérez Art Museum Miami (PAMM)

Looking out over the bay at the Downtown end of MacArthur Causeway, Herzog & de Meuron's PAMM transformed Museum Park on launch in 2013. It's a modern version of a Greek temple with a towering verandah-style entrance (above) beneath a trellised canopy supporting Patrick Blanc's hanging garden of tropical plants. Inside, within a scheme of exposed concrete and wood, the museum displays works from its permanent collection, which features Dara Friedman and Frank Stella, and a roster of temporary shows, and its shop is handy for gifts. The sculpture garden has installations by Jesús Rafael Soto and Konstantin Grcic. Closed Wednesdays. Sharing a plaza behind it is Grimshaw's Frost Museum of Science, with a golf ball-like planetarium, opened in 2017. *1103 Biscayne Boulevard, T 305 375 3000, www.pamm.org*

13.00 The Standard Spa

This 1957 building, originally designed by Norman Giller, was transformed into the serene Standard (T 305 673 1717) in 2005. As with the nearby Mondrian (T 305 514 1500), it faces Biscayne Bay, which some say is the 'wrong way', but since opening it has silenced naysayers, no doubt mollified by an afternoon spent at the spa. Interiors have a minimalist, airy, Scandinavian feel; slatted ash clads the entrance hall (above), referencing the wood of Nordic saunas. This is a sanctum for hydro-based therapies. Loll about in the marble hammam and detoxify in the pastel-hued mud baths before a dip in the arctic plunge pool and hot tub under the palms. But first of all, have a healthy lunch, perhaps the bloody veggie burger, at The Lido Bayside Grill (T 786 245 0880). *40 Island Avenue, T 305 704 3945, www.standardhotels.com*

16.30 The Bass

Bringing some much-needed culture to the beach, The Bass continues to shine under curator Silvia Karman Cubiñá, who took the reins in 2008. It did not have an auspicious birth, opening in 1964 with a collection of eccentric pieces, including tapestries and Renaissance and Baroque paintings, 77 of which were later found to be fake (classic Miami). It's still housed in architect Russell Pancoast's stately 1930 library, whose art deco stone facade is adorned with Gustav Boland's seagull sculptures and bas-reliefs, extended by Arata Isozaki in 2001 and then again in 2017 when David Gauld grew the space by roofing over two courtyards. Now it grabs headlines with contemporary art: rotating shows by the likes of Karen Rifas ('Deceptive Constructions', above) and Ugo Rondinone, who left a rainbow totem pole outside after the museum's reinauguration. *2100 Collins Avenue, T 305 673 7530, www.thebass.org*

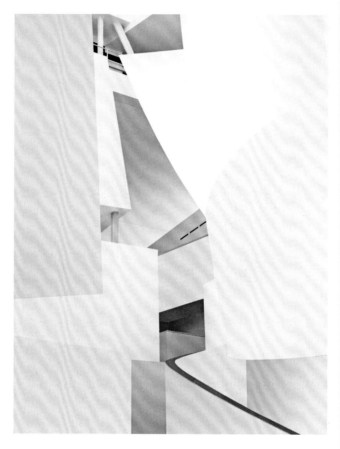

19.00 New World Center

Don't expect titanium or brushed stainless steel here – when Frank Gehry's plans for a 12,375 sq m home for the New World Symphony were unveiled, critics called them boring, boxy and utilitarian. In fact, its flat white exterior walls are used as a 650 sq m blank canvas for transmissions of performances that can be watched from a park designed by Rotterdam firm West 8 and even seen from some of the hotels on Collins Avenue. Inside the high-tech, multimedia facility, the 750-seat concert hall is defined by giant, sail-like acoustic panels, which are also used as projection surfaces. The atrium (above) is broken up into a series of geometric shapes. This is a reversal of previous Gehry buildings, in that it entertains from the inside out. *500 17th Street, T 305 680 5866, www.nws.edu*

21.00 Stubborn Seed

The 2016 winner of TV show *Top Chef* and graduate of Jean-Georges Vongerichten's Matador Room at the Edition (see p021), Jeremy Ford made this assured debut in 2017. His molecular wizardry transforms regional as well as global ingredients into superb artistic creations typified by butter-poached lobster with green curry foam, caramelised cauliflower and crispy garlic; and nairagi with gelatinous sea grapes, fermented chilli, buttermilk, kombu and pear. Celano Design Studio have dressed the 70-cover room with textured and raw materials including concrete, white tiles, exposed ducts and light bulbs and art deco-style soft furnishings and motifs. A custom-made chef's table positioned by a window affords a view of the magic in the kitchen. *101 Washington Avenue, T 786 322 5211, www.stubbornseed.com*

URBAN LIFE

CAFÉS, RESTAURANTS, BARS AND NIGHTCLUBS

Food here has improved beyond recognition, although in SoBe you may feel you're paying for the privilege of who's in the restaurant rather than what is on your plate. Then again, the point of Miami is being in the right place and being seen by the right people.

In this body-conscious city, dishes tend to be bikini-friendly, with an emphasis on fish, as at Mignonette (see p053), and fusion, as at Three at Wynwood Arcade (see p052). Cuban cooking will have you sinking like a stone, but is deep-fried delicious and perfect for hangovers – try Puerto Sagua (700 Collins Avenue, T 305 673 1115). Healthier are a slew of vegan arrivals with similar names – Plant (see p047), Planta (opposite) and Plnthouse (2341 Collins Avenue, T 305 604 6881). Haute Asian cuisine is still on trend, and Makoto (Bal Harbour Shops, T 305 864 8600) and Sushi Erika (1700 79th Street Causeway, T 786 216 7216) are two of the best exponents.

High-rolling hedonists flock to hotel bars, pool parties (see p057) and clubs such as Wall (see p026), Liv (4441 Collins Avenue, T 305 674 4680) and E11even (29 NE 11th Street, T 786 460 4803). But it's not all about flashing cash and flesh. Treasured dives Churchill's (5501 NE 2nd Avenue, T 305 757 1807) and Mac's Club Deuce (222 14th Street, T 305 531 6200) have been swelled by hip drinking dens including Broken Shaker at the Freehand (see p016), The Anderson (see p031), Bodega (see p054) and Sweet Liberty (see p056). *For full addresses, see Resources.*

Planta

Nightclub mogul David Grutman is building his rapidly expanding culinary empire with a sprinkling of stardust – and this nouveau vegan restaurant, sushi bar and cocktail lounge, launched in 2018 at the southern tip of SoBe, is no exception. It's not unusual to see Pharrell Williams or the Hadid sisters perched on one of Bend's recycled copper-coated 'Lucy' stools devouring a nigiri roll. The venue is split into a refurbished 'barn' and a contemporary glass and black-steel box with a planted concrete roof used to cultivate much of the produce. A weekend brunch of banana pancakes, falafel tacos or gluten-free pizza with a nutrient-rich Drop the Beet cocktail (mezcal, raspberries, lemon, chilli, beetroot juice and ginger) will have you back to your best quick sharp.
850 Commerce Street, T 305 397 8513, www.plantarestaurants.com

Alter

A kitchen rebel with a sustainability cause, Bradley Kilgore works with ingredients that most local chefs wouldn't dream of putting in a pan. His sophisticated creations are cunningly crafted from Floridian produce regularly spurned by other restaurants, for instance rabbit, lamb neck, cactus or grouper cheeks, which might be served with nori *nage* and shoyu hollandaise. The barely poached egg with sea scallop foam, truffle pearls and caviar is one of the few regulars on a list of 'enhancements' that can be added to the seasonal five- or seven-course tasting menus. Unpolished interiors – tables made from salvaged barn doors and a distressed paint effect by the street artist Me She – reinforce the culinary philosophy. Dinner only. Closed Mondays. *223 NW 23rd Street, T 305 573 5996, www.altermiami.com*

Sherwood's Bistro & Bar

Known for her homely Wynwood eaterie Morgan's (T 305 573 9678), trend-setting Barclay Graebner has done it again with this neighbourhood bistro in Little River, which arrived in 2017. In a former medical centre painted in dusty pink and intense blue, interiors by business partner Steve Harivel exude an eccentric vibe – a deco bar thrown out in The Raleigh renovation, tin ceilings from a Kentucky school, tiles from a Lisbon embassy and a Dylan Egon mural. The eclectic menu encompasses a milk and honey platter, local snapper, pork ramen, sweet potato and coconut curry and banana pudding with cookies and salted caramel, and cocktails feature small-batch liquor. In 2019, food hall The Citadel (T 305 908 3849) launched nearby in an old bank. *8281 NE 2nd Avenue, T 786 359 4030, www.sherwoodsbistro.com*

Amara at Paraiso

The prolific Michael Schwartz (see p020) nailed it here with Miami's first top-notch waterfront restaurant, set in the shadow of Paraiso Bay – four Arquitectonica condos with bubbled facades that put Edgewater on the map in 2018. Meyer Davis created a beach club vibe with blondwood, graphic aquamarine tiles, white furnishings and tropical prints. The menu celebrates the city's Latin roots and goes straight to its collective stomach with yuca cheese puffs that engender fits of nostalgia, ceviches, feijoada and a wood-grill Argentine meat fest that includes hanger steak, short ribs and green chorizo. Kick off the Manolos and stick your toes in the sand at happy hour, or come on Sundays for oysters, skewers and cocktails at the sunset party on the terrace. *3101 NE 7th Avenue, T 305 702 5528, www.amaraatparaiso.com*

Upland

Nestled in the epicurean triangle south of fifth with Stubborn Steed (see p039) and Planta (see p041), this duplicate of Justin Smillie's New York hit works as well as the original. The chef's upbringing in rural US and immersion in Italian kitchens informs his philosophy, and headline dishes are slow-cooked in coal- and wood-fired BBQ ovens – roast salmon with red grapefruit, pickled beets and farro salad, and short rib for two with olives, walnuts and celery, sides of charred broccoli with tahini, and pizzas like sausage and kale. Roman and Williams decked it out with copper-piping shelves, darkwood, Prussian-green leather booths and some very Californian back-lit lemons. Open for dinner only, as well as a weekend brunch with bottomless Mimosas. *49 Collins Avenue, T 305 602 9998, www.uplandmiami.com*

Plant

This vegan and kosher restaurant is part of The Sacred Space, a wellness retreat that hosts yoga and meditation and places itself on a different plane to all the bars and *bulla* in Wynwood. For launch in 2017, architect Rene Gonzalez (see p082) gifted one of his own 40-year-old palm trees to elevate the feng shui water feature in the patio garden and installed arty site-specific strip lighting and a kitchen large enough to offer cooking classes. Many of the ingredients, including 67 varieties of edible flowers, come from its organic Florida pantry, Paradise Farms. Executive chef Horacio Rivadero uses them in super-food bowls and salads, and dishes like fennel ceviche, sous vide mushroom *ropa vieja* and jackfruit tacos; to drink there are craft cocktails and biodynamic wines. *105 NE 24th Street, T 305 814 5365, www.plantmiami.com*

Chotto Matte

An outpost of London Nikkei eaterie and cocktail bar Chotto Matte moved in on 1111 Lincoln Road (see p010) turf (the mixed-use white box is also the work of Herzog & de Meuron) with a swagger in 2018. Architects AMA have thrown every design trick in the book at it. Behind a huge pivoting entrance wall is a cenote-inspired grotto clad in shou sugi ban and graffiti by locals Marcel Katz and Ahol Sniffs Glue, illuminated via a retractable roof above palms and hanging gardens by the wonderfully monikered Raymond Jungles, and a 21-ton lava boulder. Soak up the scene at the bar and cherry-pick from the robata, tempura, sautée and sushi menus with a Fuji Highball (Suntory Toki, mint, soda water and edible flower). *1664 Lenox Avenue, T 305 690 0743, www.chotto-matte.com/miami*

Casa Tua

Should you intend to impress a local, Casa Tua is the place to reserve – especially if you snag an outside table. The restaurant is nicely hidden from the road by a hedge surrounding a pretty garden, which wraps around two sides of the Mediterranean-style villa. The atmosphere is low-key but the waiters are attentive, which is quite a welcome change from the usual SoBe attitude. The food is northern Italian, with a few twists, and the results are delicious. Casa Tua is always packed and regulars are rewarded with an upstairs club that is members-only on weekends. Don't let that put you off, though – try a firm telephone manner, or book one of the five charming, cosy suites in the boutique hotel (T 305 673 0973), designed by Michele Bonan. *1700 James Avenue, T 305 673 1010, www.casatualifestyle.com*

Three at Wynwood Arcade

After a seven-year spell upstate, Norman Van Aken, one of the fathers of New World Cuisine (Latin, African and Asian fusion), returned as anchor for this restaurant and retail complex that cemented Wynwood's coming of age in 2017. Art now almost plays second fiddle to all the high-end dining and drinking venues, although here, Tristan Eaton's asymmetrical murals decorate the cast-iron facade. Aken's menu stays true to his roots, typified by slow-roast venison with cauliflower and coconut-cream kale, and the *paella nueva*, with triple tail, butter-poached clams and chorizo Ibérico – very Miami. Dinner and weekend brunch only. At casual rooftop bar No 3 Social, try the Cactus Flower cocktail mixed with mezcal, aloe liquor, lemon, agave and prosecco. *50 NW 24th Street, T 305 748 4540, www.threewynwood.com*

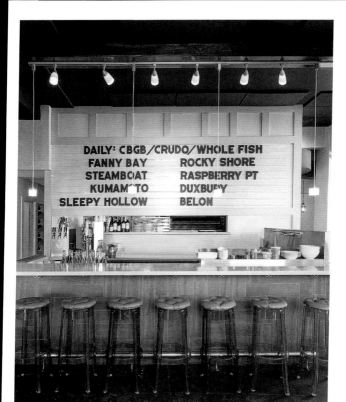

DAILY: CBGB/CRUDO/WHOLE FISH
FANNY BAY   ROCKY SHORE
STEAMBOAT   RASPBERRY PT
KUMAMOTO   DUXBURY
SLEEPY HOLLOW   BELON

Mignonette

The owner of this oyster bar in a 1930s gas station, Daniel Serfer, gained acclaim for his comfort food at Blue Collar (T 305 756 0366) in the MiMo area. Here, he invades Edgewater, another part of town that was lacking in decent eateries, although Amara at Paraiso (see p045) has since swelled the local ranks. Oyster varieties are listed on a cinema letter board and paired with the namesake sauce; throwbacks include shrimp cocktail and clams casino; and there is a lobster roll, a daily chowder, a seafood tower, an Osetra caviar plate and all manner of sautéed vegetables. Copper mobiles and globe pendants dangle from above and caramel banquettes skirt a brick wall. It looks out to a cemetery, which gives green respite along this industrial stretch. *210 NE 18th Street, T 305 374 4635, www.mignonettemiami.com*

Bodega Taqueria y Tequila

It may look like just another late-night Tex-Mex serving from a tricked-out food truck but push an innocuous door to discover a double-height deconstructed warehouse behind that gets packed with a sassy crowd at weekends or when there is a live band. There are a few artworks by Mr Brainwash but the main feature is the elongated bar from which bottles of Dos Equis, shots of aguardiente, overproof bourbon and Don Julio 1942, served with orange zest and ground cinnamon, and kick-ass cocktails mixed with the likes of Ilegal mezcal, flow freely. Juicy tacos, from pork and pineapple to steak chimichurri and avocado and black beans, as well as *antojitos* and burritos, are on offer until 4am every night to keep you from falling off your Tabouret stool. *1220 16th Street, T 305 704 2145, www.bodegasouthbeach.com*

Sweet Liberty

Master mixologist John Lermeyer's legend was forged when he teamed up with Lenny Kravitz in the seminal Florida Room at the height of the Delano's (see p029) pomp in 2007. None of the young pretenders, among them Broken Shaker (see p040), Lost Boy (T 305 372 7303) and Mama Tried (T 786 803 8087), have bettered his ingenious concoctions, such as the Sweet Potato Pain Killer (three rums, coconut cream, sweet potato juice, orange juice and allspice) here at his final creation. It's a late-night haunt with a diner-inspired design by Deft Union featuring neon and palm-print wallpaper. Midnight snacks like lobster 'hot pocket', cauliflower steak and grilled bone marrow, and a free-wheeling soundtrack, keep the good-looking crowd well stoked until 5am. *237 20th Street, T 305 763 8217, www.mysweetliberty.com*

Hyde Beach

This east coast outpost of Hyde on Sunset Strip, with interiors by Philippe Starck, has been inserted into the SLS Hotel. The 2012 wood-panelled addition to L Murray Dixon's 1939 building cantilevers over the pool on pillars, and there's plenty more wood inside and a long bar, but the fun is most intense out on the deck and around Starck's huge duck. We prefer the Sunday afternoon vibe; on Thursdays and weekends, it turns into a fully fledged nightclub with DJs until 2am. Note that even during the day, women wear heels with bikinis (and at night, dance with arms above heads as champagne sprays). Facing the bay, The Mondrian (T 305 514 1500) is one of the few hotels with a sunset view and its Sunday parties turn the pool pink and get the crowd rowdy on rosé. *1701 Collins Avenue (enter on 17th Street), T 305 455 2990, www.hydebeach.com*

Kyu

Jean-Georges Vongerichten's Matador Room at the Edition (see p021) has been a prolific breeding ground for the city's most exciting young chefs, notably Jeremy Ford at Stubborn Seed (see p039) and Michael Lewis here. His wood-fired Asian-inspired debut is a treat for all the senses. Set back from Wynwood's main drag, it's signposted by 2 Alas' mural at the entrance (opposite). The grey shed is warmed by bespoke wood furniture by local outfit HabibCo and art by Stefan Rohrer and Christian Klugman. Lewis works wonders on the grill in dishes including duck breast 'burnt ends', Wagyu brisket, and roast cauliflower with goat's cheese and shishito; the pork and shitake gyoza with smoked truffle ponzu is equally divine. For every tree burnt, Kyu plants five. *251 NW 25th Street, T 786 577 0150, www.kyurestaurants.com*

Juvia

Jonas and Alexandra Millan's penthouse is the only SoBe eaterie worth reserving for its view, and Patricia Urquiola's 'Crinoline' chairs are the most coveted date seats in Miami. Venezuelan architect Alejandro Barrios-Carrero invited Patrick Blanc to add some green to the purple theme and his verdant vertical garden, and a water feature that's lit up at night, freshens up the roof deck. Executive chef Sunny Oh's exquisite Franco-Nikkei dishes (roquefort terrine with greens, walnut and apricots; yellowtail *tiradito*, mint and puffed rice; rock shrimp *acevichado*; and seared tuna with caramelised shallots) live up to the setting. Or settle in at the amethyst bar for a colour-coded Juvia 2.0 made with gin, beet juice, raspberry, lemon and ginger.
1111 Lincoln Road, T 305 763 8272, www.juviamiami.com

MC Kitchen

The 4141 building in the Design District is home to prestige brands including Flos, Maxalto, Acerbis and Lema, as well as this restrained Italian restaurant turning out truffle fries, pear and four cheese *fiocchi*, and poulet rouge with roasted marble potatoes, pearl onions and pepperoncini pan jus. The subtle beige- and grey-toned interiors are enlivened by the whimsical sunflower-yellow sculpture (above) that takes flight from the wood panelling. Do not be disappointed if the only space is at the marble counter surrounding the open kitchen. It is a fine place to eavesdrop on designers talking shop, enjoy an *affogato* (served in a champagne glass with a scoop of caramel gelato and homemade biscotti) and grab a few words with chef Victor Toro. *4141 NE 2nd Avenue, T 305 456 9948, www.mckitchenmiami.com*

INSIDER'S GUIDE

KARLA FERGUSON-SOIMAUD, GALLERIST

Jamaican-born Karla Ferguson adopted Miami as her home and dived into the art scene in 2006. She says she was inspired to 'help people discover the hodgepodge flavour that represents our city. You can immerse yourself in so many different cultures here.' Her Yeelen Group space in Little Haiti is a haven for artists focused on racial and LGBT rights. She's a regular at nearby The Fountainhead Residency (690 NE 56th Street), which 'attracts cutting-edge global names', and Laundromat Art Space (5900 NE 2nd Avenue, T 305 375 0001), and visits Locust Projects (3852 N Miami Avenue, T 305 576 8570) – 'it's diverse, and puts on great speakers' – and PAMM (see p034), since director Franklin Sirmans broadened the outlook.

Ferguson shops at The Webster (see p091) and in the Design District, where 'you can find affordable boutiques', such as Mrs Mandolin (4218 NE 2nd Avenue, T 786 420 5110) and the pop-ups at leafy complex Upper Buena Vista (184 NE 50th Terrace, T 305 539 9555). She eats at Seven Seas Restaurant & Fish Market (5205 NE 2nd Avenue, T 305 981 3571) for the 'Dominican comfort food' and is a fan of the BYOB vibe at Ironside Kitchen Pizza & Coffee Co (7580 NE 4th Court, T 305 531 5055). Her new favourite restaurants are Chotto Matte (see p048) and 'sexy' Swan (90 NE 39th Street, T 305 704 0994). Afterwards, if it's a night out, she might well head to the Edition (see p021), which has a 'cool basement party'.
For full addresses, see Resources.

ART AND DESIGN
GALLERIES, STUDIOS AND PUBLIC SPACES

Miami has always been a voracious consumer of design. However, the majority of it hails from elsewhere. Model residences, from the Tudor, Chinese or French 'villages' of Coral Gables to multiple MiMo apartments, required furnishing. Launched in 1959, Arango (5864 Sunset Drive, T 305 661 4229) still exists, as does Luminaire (2331 Ponce de Leon Boulevard, T 305 448 7367), but along with the more recent arrivals (see p070), they are all dominated by imports.

Similarly with art. Among others, Craig Robins (see p032), the Bramans (opposite) and the Rubells (see p066) brought Art Basel to the city back in 2002. Visitors discovered the many superb private museums (see p076) and the excitement firmly connected the idea of Miami and art in the media. Yet, despite the feverish nature of the market, little deserving of global attention is actually created here.

Homegrown and locally based talent does exist, from sculptor Michele Oka Doner to painter Hernan Bas, artist Michelle Weinberg, Daniel Arsham, whose work straddles architecture and performance, designer Laz Ojalde and Cuban Alexandre Arrechea, an ex-member of Los Carpinteros. Seek out the new generation at ArtCenter/South Florida (924 Lincoln Road, T 305 674 8278), a studio complex that opens its doors in the afternoons, although the city is still more likely to give us actors, singers or wide receivers. That said, as there's now more support than ever for the arts, the situation is sure to improve. *For full addresses, see Resources.*

Public sculpture

As approaching Miami by sea is so popular, sculpture is often set close to the water, partly thanks to the Art in Public Places initiative, which demands set-asides from construction budgets, and partly because owners simply like to show off. Norman and Irma Braman have so many pieces on their Indian Creek Island lawn, it is often mistaken for a gallery. At the cruise ship terminal, John Henry's constructivist *Je*

Souhaite (above) is painted an intense blue that rivals the colour of the sky and, at 24m high, serves as a beacon for liners coming into port. However, the city's best collection is located quite some way inland – Martin Margulies (see p076) displays work by Joan Miró, Isamu Noguchi, Willem de Kooning et al on the Florida International University campus (11200 SW 8th Street).
N Cruise Boulevard, Cruise Ship Dock

Rubell Museum

Prolific collectors Donald and Mera Rubell, son Jason and daughter Jennifer, flit from global fairs to studios, acquiring hundreds of pieces a year by young and mid-career artists. Through Donald's brother, Steve Rubell, co-founder of Studio 54, they were in with the New York scene from the 1970s and own many works by Keith Haring, Jean-Michel Basquiat and Cindy Sherman, who was a regular guest for dinner. Since 1993, excerpts of the stockpile ('New Aquisitions', above) have been rotated in a former Drug Enforcement Agency impound in Wynwood (neatly summing up the story of Miami). In late 2019 the Rubell is crossing Interstate 95 to a vast 7,500 sq m 'campus' (1100 NW 23rd Street) with a garden, restaurant and library in gritty, up-and-coming Allapattah. *95 NW 29th Street, T 305 573 6090, www.rfc.museum*

Nina Johnson

Prominent Wynwood figure Nina Johnson's move north to Little Haiti after rising rents forced her to pull the plug on Gallery Diet, which opened in 2007 to support emerging artists, many of whom went on to establish global reputations, heralds a seismic shift in the Miami scene. Interiors firm Charlap Hyman & Herrero have converted a 1940s compound encompassing a storefront that was once a church (into the main space), a two-storey house (into two more galleries) and another building (now a residence for artists), set in a garden of mango, oak and avocado trees. It puts on shows by exciting locals such as Jamilah Sabur, who mainly works with burlap and plaster, and other young talent including Brooklyn conceptual designer Katie Stout ('Narcissus', above). *6315 NW 2nd Avenue, T 305 571 2288, www.ninajohnson.com*

Museum Garage

Ever since 1111 Lincoln Road (see p010) exploded the notion of the drab car park, developers have been trying to emulate the feat. This outlandish effort takes the concept to a flamboyant new high. Craig Robins called on Terence Riley, who threw the dice, assembling five firms including Nicolas Buffe, Workac and his own practice K/R to each conceive part of a patchwork exterior. J Mayer H wrapped the corner of the seven-storey concrete structure with jigsaw-like 'XOX' blobs (left), while Clavel took a more literal interpretation with its 'Urban Jam' metallic car motif. Elsewhere, seek out OMA's Faena Park (Collins Avenue/35th Street), which has a perforated facade that reveals its high-tech stacking system in action, and Park@420 (Drexel Avenue/16th Street) by Ten Arquitectos, for its mix of square apertures and art deco curves.
NE 1st Avenue/NE 41st Street,
www.miamidesigndistrict.net

Nisi B Home

Owner Nisi Berryman is inordinately fond of Murano glass, malachite and brilliant colours, and her window displays positively glow. She was a Design District pioneer, purveying furniture, lighting, accessories, textiles and artwork to discerning buyers. We were taken by Christopher Gentner's brass and blackened-steel 'Dischi Table', Marco Lorenzetto's expansive abstract pattern paintings and Luis Pons' 'Frame Collection Dresser' (above), made to order using picture mouldings. Pons was born in Venezuela and emigrated here (as have many of his compatriots) in 2003, and his own studio (T 305 576 1787) is a few blocks away. Nisi B often hosts parties honouring local creatives such as Michele Oka Doner, Benjamin Noriega-Ortiz and Simon Chaput. *39 NE 39th Street, T 305 573 1939, www.nisibhome.com*

Art Nouveau Gallery

Many galleries represent Latin American artists but Art Nouveau stands out for its focus on geometric abstraction. Its HQ is in Maracaibo, and it champions legendary Venezuelans Jesús Rafael Soto and Carlos Cruz-Diez, as well as Milton Becerra, who works with looms and found materials like rocks to create intricate structural forms that are inspired by his indigenous heritage ('Wale'kerü: Líneas de Luz', above). Other highlights of its collection have been Carlos Medina's polymer sculptures that resemble sheets of folded paper, welded iron wings by Lía Bermudez, Héctor Ramírez's kinetic spheres, and kaleidoscopic op art by Arturo Quintero. Cuban painters Pedro de Oraá, Waldo Díaz-Balart and José María Mijares also make up a large part of the roster. *348 NW 29th Street, T 305 573 4661, www.artnouveau-gallery.com*

Fredric Snitzer Gallery
Stalwart Fredric Snitzer started selling posters to cocaine cowboys in the 1980s and has championed Latino artists, such as Carlos Alfonzo and Rafael Domench, ever since. His switch from Coral Gables to Wynwood in 2004 helped catapult the enclave into the limelight. The stable now includes Alice Aycock, Kenny Scharf and Tomas Vu ('The Fifth Season', pictured). *1540 NE Miami Court, T 305 448 8976*

Institute of Contemporary Art

A home for the ICA in the Design District represents a coming of age for the retail paradise. Madrid architects Aranguren + Gallegos gave the three-storey building a geometric metallic facade that tries its best to wrest attention from the peacocking of the luxe stores in the immediate vicinity. The rear glass-clad exterior looks out over a sculpture garden, which hosts pieces by George Segal, and happenings such as Judy Chicago's smoke performance that was the centrepiece of her 2019 retrospective, 'A Reckoning'. The permanent collection has work by late 20th-century US and global artists including Manuel Solano, Chris Ofili and Sondra Perry ('Typhoon Coming On', opposite), as well as paintings by Miami-based Hernan Bas. Tuesdays to Sundays.
61 NE 41st Street, T 305 901 5272, www.icamiami.org

De la Cruz and Margulies Collections

In a three-floor venue as big as the Met Breuer, the de la Cruz Collection is one of Miami's highlights (works by Cosima von Bonin, Allora & Calzadilla and Lucy McKenzie, pictured). It's strong on Latino and US artists, debuting works by Tauba Auerbach, Wade Guyton, Rashid Johnson and Glenn Ligon, and exhibiting unique collections by the likes of Felix Gonzalez-Torres and Christopher Wool. Adjacent to Interstate 95, The Margulies Collection is another must-see, showing pieces by Sol LeWitt, Willem de Kooning and Richard Serra; Gilles Barbier's darkly humorous *L'Hospice* depicts a superheroes' nursing home. It opened in 1999, before an arts district in Wynwood was even a concept. *De La Cruz, 23 NE 41st Street, T 305 576 6112; Margulies, 591 NW 27th Street, T 305 576 1051*

Emmett Moore

Miami native Emmett Moore is yet another creative to have moved out to Little River, where he set up his studio inside a disused mall. His work blurs sculpture, design and furniture-making, regularly mixing formal craftsmanship with repurposed quotidian objects and a dose of wit – plywood faux-fire extinguishers; garden loungers made of cinder blocks; and an ashtray crafted from resin-cast cigarette butts. 'Palm Tropical Depression' (above) was a campy homage to the silhouette so often seen in Miami's neon signs, reinterpreted in steel rod and concrete, while a series of rugs for heritage firm Odabashian featured marble, granite or terrazzo patterns laid over messed-up geometries, and his 'Zither Table' calls to mind Noguchi and Rietveld's work. Pieces are sold through Nina Johnson (see p067). *www.emmettmoore.com*

Wynwood Walls

Credit developer Tony Goldman for seeing a forgotten area of decrepit warehouses, Salvation Army stores, modest residences, chain-link fences and stray dogs as a future arts hub. He began snapping up property in the 2000s and, knowing that paint is the cheapest real-estate cosmetic fix, curated and organised the graffiti artists who were already tagging buildings. The result is a riot of painted walls, often intricate work by renowned names like LA-based Retna (above, at 250 NW 23rd Street) and local Johnny Robles, who is represented by the Robert Fontaine Gallery (T 305 397 8530). The pièce de résistance is Wynwood Walls (2520 NW 2nd Avenue; open 11am to 11pm, Sundays 12pm to 6pm), an enclosed garden with murals recreated for every Art Basel. Goldman's children now run the project. *www.thewynwoodwalls.com*

ARCHITOUR

A GUIDE TO MIAMI'S ICONIC BUILDINGS

Miami's architecture is defined by its periods of prosperity. In the 1920s, developers built Mediterranean revival homes by the sea, but then came the crash in 1929. It was followed by the art deco hotels and banks of the 1930s and 1940s, with their ziggurats, flat roofs, convex corners and geometric patterns – take a stroll along Ocean Drive from 5th Street to The Raleigh (1775 Collins Avenue). MiMo (opposite) reflected postwar optimism and celebrated car culture in roadside motels such as Norman Giller's 1953 New Yorker (6500 Biscayne Boulevard, T 305 759 5823) and the Vagabond (see p030). A more restrained midcentury style and cheap land brought ranch houses and glass-walled, linear residences, as well as the singular Marine Stadium (see p084) and Bacardi Complex (see p086).

From the late 1980s, the city was infested by humdrum condos, their primary attribute being security. Some exceptions were by Arquitectonica, which made its name with the 1978 Pink House (9325 N Bayshore Drive), Atlantis (see p014) and the American Airlines Arena (601 Biscayne Boulevard) in 1999. In recent times, starchitects have created pied-à-terres for the mega-rich (see p082). More interestingly, Tony Goldman's successful Wynwood formula (see p079) is being copy-pasted elsewhere as developers kickstart new cultural quarters – affordable rents are attracting creatives in Little River, Little Haiti, the MiMo District, Allapattah and Hialeah. *For full addresses, see Resources.*

MiMo architecture

The art deco district mirrored the age of ocean travel. Then, a few decades later, MiMo (Miami Modern) was inextricably linked with the car. The main route into the city becomes Biscayne Boulevard, along which sprouted flashy motels including the Vagabond (see p030), boasting atomic and starburst signs blinking in neon, decorative brise-soleil, biomorphic pools and organic cantilevered roofs. Examples of the style can be seen from NE 50th to 77th Street, at Biscayne Plaza Shopping Center (NE 79th Street) and on Bay Harbor Islands, notably the 1957 Mediterranean Apartments (9101 E Bay Harbor Drive; above), a fan-shaped block sheathed in white concrete lattice designed by Herbert Mathes. Also check out the genius of Morris Lapidus, especially the 1954 Fontainebleau hotel (4441 Collins Avenue), with its distinctive cheese holes.

Glass

No fewer than seven Pritzker Prize winners have joined the luxury residence gold rush since 2015. Richard Meier (see p022), Rem Koolhaas, Foster + Partners, Renzo Piano, Zaha Hadid, Herzog & de Meuron and Jean Nouvel have all made hay in the Sunshine State. Yet none outshine these beautifully understated 18 storeys by the homegrown Rene Gonzalez. The last condo tower to be permitted in desirable SoFi, it comprises just 10 full-floor apartments including a triplex penthouse with 360-degree views, and is blessed with the wonderful detailing that has become his trademark. The panels of the wraparound balconies have a vertical frit pattern that reduces in density as the building rises to conjure a feeling of levity, and the windows reflect the sky in the day and radiate golden hues at dawn and dusk. *120 Ocean Drive, www.glasssouthbeach.com*

United States Post Office

During the Depression, the Government threw cash at public works, including this still-functioning post office. But don't come for the stamps. The streamline moderne building by Howard Cheney opened in 1937 with a breathtaking two-storey rotunda (its domed ceiling symbolises the sun and sky), a fountain and wraparound gold mailboxes. A triptych mural by local painter Charles Russell Hardman, which was installed a few years later, depicts Ponce de León's discovery of Florida; Seminoles attacking DeSoto; and a confrontation between the Indians and the US Army. Two blocks south is the Mediterranean revival old City Hall (1130 Washington Avenue) built, defiantly, in 1927, a year after a hurricane levelled most of Miami Beach. A cinematheque in its lobby shows arthouse films.
1300 Washington Avenue

Miami Marine Stadium

This elongated MiMo stadium, built along the Rickenbacker Causeway in 1963, once sat 6,500 people. They came in droves to see powerboat races, waterskiing, flotillas and regattas, or concerts (Sammy Davis Jr, The Who), religious services and boxing matches staged on a floating barge, often surrounded by hundreds of boats, against a backdrop of Downtown across the bay. Designed by Cuban-born architect Hilario Candela when he was just 27, the expansive swoop of concrete bleachers is sheltered by a cantilevered folded-plate canopy. It was abandoned in 1992 after being battered by Hurricane Andrew, but a campaign to get it listed was successful and the city hopes to restore this aquatic hippodrome. The site is officially off-limits but fishermen, graffiti artists and skateboarders find their way in. *Rickenbacker Causeway, Virginia Key*

Bacardi Complex

Enrique Gutierrez's eight-storey block of tropical modernism for Bacardi (the rum company and architect were both Cuban exiles) was unveiled in 1963. Its sides are clad with 28,000 hand-painted, cartoony azulejo tiles depicting exotic flora designed by Brazilian Francisco Brennand. Gutierrez was a Mies van der Rohe protégé, and the raised plaza, glass curtain walls and core structure show his influence. Local Ignacio Carrera-Justiz's exquisite annex (above), a cantilevered box of glass 'tapestries' based on abstract paintings of sugarcane and bats by Johannes Dietz, was added in 1975. By 2009, Bacardi had outgrown the site and consolidated operations in Coral Gables. It was bought by the YoungArts Foundation, who installed galleries and a performance space by Frank Gehry, yet it is the complex itself that remains the best work of art.
2100 Biscayne Boulevard, T 305 377 1140, www.youngarts.org

SHOPS
THE BEST RETAIL THERAPY AND WHAT TO BUY

The best global fashion (Brunello Cucinelli, Etro, Roberto Cavalli) still clusters in Bal Harbour Shops (9700 Collins Avenue, T 305 866 0311) and there's an illustrious coterie of big brands in the Design District (see p033) and Brickell City Centre (see p009). Yet Miami's creative pulse is quickening, although you'll have to actively seek it out, as the most interesting concepts, such as Fabrice Tardieu (see p095), are putting down roots in Wynwood (opposite), Little River (see p090) and other proliferating pockets of hip, in search of lower rents, more space and a less fickle crowd. Swimwear stalwart Trina Turk (7200 Biscayne Boulevard, T 786 409 4383) has set up in MiMo central (see p030) and Karelle Levy's hip knitwear label Krelwear is among more than 60 showrooms, galleries and pop-ups at nearby Miami Ironside (7520 NE 4th Court, T 305 528 2755; by appointment). Also on Biscayne Boulevard, Logan Real (www.loganreal.com) has gained a cult following for his bespoke hand-painted leather items.

The city is also known for its wealth of midcentury gems, from ashtrays shaped like rockets to Valentino dresses, while Paul Evans' copper, brass and steel pieces, and Murano glass birds, end up here in large numbers, inexplicably. Treasures await at Vermillion (765 NE 125th Street, T 305 893 7800), which stockpiles furniture and lighting from the 1930s to the 1990s, and Déjà Vu Décor (117 NE 54th Street, T 305 972 8200), a great source for 1950s and 1960s icons. *For full addresses, see Resources.*

Base Superstore

Steven Giles, Base's creative director, has become quite the tastemaker. After more than two decades on Lincoln Road, where he set up in 1994 and went on to pioneer experiential lifestyle retail, he moved his HQ from SoBe to Wynwood in 2017. Giles now runs the consultancy side, including a collaboration with Ian Schrager at the Edition (see p021) and Base is overseen by his business partner Bruce Cannella. The emporium purveys men's clothing with a focus on emerging brands, and stocks an eclectic range of streetwear, sneakers, accessories and grooming products. Look out for jewellery by local designers Luis Morais and Miansai, skateboard decks by Anitya Fantôme and Base's own scents. You do not so much shop here as join a cult.
2215 NW 2nd Avenue, T 305 531 4982, www.baseworld.com

4510/Six

Founded in Los Angeles, this concept store transplanted to Miami in 2018, offering an antidote to trashy beachwear. The stylish low-slung Little River space fuses existing industrial elements with cheer: huge round mirrors, fringed fitting-room curtains in sunset hues, Waka Waka's birch-ply chairs, a terrazzo table by Pieces by An Aesthetic Pursuit and prints of local art deco detail by Hamish Robertson. Bubblegum-pink racks hold garments by under-the-radar US designers, including fleece sweaters by Sandy Liang, patchwork leather skirts by Lorod and metallic parkas by Nomia. Also pick up homewares like Tennen Studio's nickel-finished incense holders and the irreverent own-brand Boy Smells candles, which come in glossy black-glass tumblers. *7338 NW Miami Court, T 786 615 4700, www.fortyfiveten.com*

The Webster

French fashionista Laure Hériard Dubreuil's all-conquering multi-brand boutique and lifestyle emporium launched here in 2009, in a revamped 1939 art deco hotel designed by Henry Hohauser. The terrazzo floor is original, and further colour is injected by the tropical-print furniture by Paul Frankl, vintage wallpaper, art by Rogan Gregory, Nate Lowman, Aaron Young and Max Snow and, of course, the mens and womenswear, accessories and homewares. Come here to seek out labels including The Row, Celine, Off-White and Loewe. For that Miami look, match a LHD x Eres bikini or beachwear by Lisa Marie Fernandez with a jaunty Maison Michele fedora. The roof terrace often hosts pop-ups with an occasional bar. There's also an outlet in Bal Harbour (T 305 868 6544). *1220 Collins Avenue, T 305 674 7899, www.thewebster.us*

Small Tea
A zen tearoom is the perfect fit for boho
Coral Gables. This is a spot to escape the
coffee culture, reset and stick a pinky up
to the mad-hatters over a civilised brew
served with scientific precision. Osmose
clad it in 1,250 abaca-covered boxes and
installed Lievore Altherr Molina's 'Catifa
80' chairs. To take away are nearly 100
types of organic tea in handmade tins.
205 Aragon Avenue, T 786 401 7189

Alchemist

This fashion label created by Roma and Erika Cohen occupies a covetable space in 1111 Lincoln Road (see p010). Designed by architect Rene Gonzalez (see p082), it's a glass box high up in the car park with fine panoramas and a 48-panel mirrored ceiling by art collective Random International that 'flutters' when you linger. Hung on silver rails or artfully positioned are menswear, womenswear, bags, jewellery and shoes.

Collections often make a bold statement, such as the Americana-inspired pieces and torn orange athleisurewear. It is all manufactured using high-quality fabrics, from studded, fringed leather jackets to hand-finished couture joggers and hybrid sneaker/boots. The store stays open until 9pm – and there's plenty of parking too.
Level 5, 1111 Lincoln Road, T 305 531 4815, www.shopalchemist.com

Fabrice Tardieu

Adding swagger to Little River's flourishing retail offerings, Fabrice Tardieu's bespoke footwear attracts a celebrity clientele. His python-skin 'Maximilien' sneakers, made by hand with leather-laced eyelet detailing and signature tongue zip, have been worn by Miami Heat superstar Dwyane Wade as well as boxer Saúl 'Canelo' Álvarez. Snakes no longer need to die in order to keep Wade in pumps, as Tardieu's leathersmiths now recreate the effect in Italian workshops. The 'I am Mexico' line, a collaboration with Canelo, comes in the colours of the national flag, and the 'Emy C Graffiti Artsy' is a paint-splattered high-top with 'One Battle At A Time' emblazoned around the sole. There are velvet moccasins too, stitched with the perfectly louche phrase *'je m'en fous'*.
7221 NW 2nd Avenue, T 786 631 4194,
www.fabricetardieu.com

ESCAPES

WHERE TO GO IF YOU WANT TO LEAVE TOWN

Miami is too often thought of as nothing more than a beach resort, rather than a vibrant city surrounded by natural beauty, which is a pity. It's an easy day trip to the Vizcaya Museum & Gardens (3251 S Miami Avenue, T 305 250 9133), a 1922 *Citizen Kane*-esque folly with taste so bad, it's fabulous. And if you head north out of the city, you'll pass the Museum of Contemporary Art (770 NE 125th Street, T 305 893 6211), where Jack Pierson's *Paradise Lights*, made of Las Vegas signs, installed outside (except in hurricane season) confirms Lenny Bruce's remark that Miami is where neon goes to die. Carry on past it to Fort Lauderdale (see p101), which is on the way up; the W hotel (401 N Fort Lauderdale Beach Boulevard, T 954 414 8200) has planted the flag for luxury. Follow the I-95 further and you'll hit the pristine sands of Hugh Taylor Birch State Park, and then Palm Beach, a pocket of unthinkable wealth that has attracted two superb art museums – the Norton (1451 S Olive Avenue, T 561 832 5196) and the Flagler (1 Whitehall Way, T 561 655 2833).

Further afield are St Petersburg, home to HOK's Dali Museum (1 Dali Boulevard, T 727 823 3767), and the modernist enclave of Sarasota (see p102). Then there's the Everglades, of course. After a lifelong fight, conservationist Marjory Stoneman Douglas' 'river of grass' is now mostly protected. Beware: part of the Miami to Sarasota road is dubbed Alligator Alley – and it is no joke.

For full addresses, see Resources.

The Island House, The Bahamas

The Bahamian capital Nassau is located on New Providence, the most populous of the archipelago's 700 islands, yet it still offers pristine beaches, and offshore coral reefs excellent for scuba diving and snorkelling. Stay at The Island House, which is set on a verdant estate. Champalimaud's interiors feature pieces by Herman Miller and Knoll, 30 rooms dressed in wood and wicker, and there's a Bamford Spa, yoga studio, cinema, a pair of restaurants and a fine collection of contemporary local art. If it piques your interest, visit the National Art Gallery of The Bahamas (T 242 328 5800), housed in a dusty-yellow 1860s colonial villa, and The Current (T 242 788 8827), which sells work by accomplished native artists. There are multiple one-hour flights daily from Miami. *Mahogany Hill Western Road, Nassau, T 242 698 6300, www.the-island-house.com*

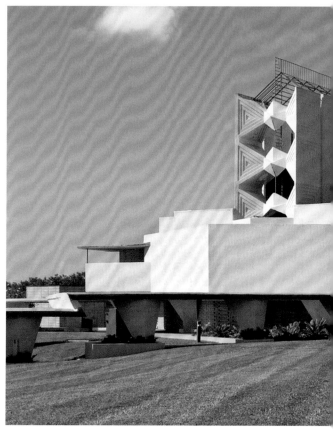

Florida Southern College, Lakeland

During The Great Depression, in 1938, the dean of Florida Southern College devised a plan to reignite enrolment, commissioning the USA's most celebrated architect, Frank Lloyd Wright, to envision a modern utopia that would garner global recognition. He conceived 18 structures, 12 of which came to fruition over 20 years. The Annie Pfeiffer Chapel (above) was both the first and most elaborate project; a multi-layered concrete ensemble of canopies and cantilevers with a soaring monolith of geometric cut-outs and wrought-iron webbing bursting out of the middle. A 13th building, Usonian House, was added in 2013 in line with the original design (Wright's early Prairie style). There are daily tours. To get here, it's a one-hour flight to Tampa and then a 45-minute drive. *Visitor Centre, 840 Johnson Avenue, T 863 680 4597, www.flsouthern.edu*

Stiltsville

One mile south of Cape Florida, Stiltsville is a motley group of wood huts supported on piles driven into the shallow flats, built offshore to circumvent Prohibition in the 1930s. There were once 27 shacks, forming a watery playground of gambling and illicit liquor. Only seven have managed to survive the hurricanes over the years; there are plans to turn them into artists' residences and marine park offices. To visit, befriend a boat owner, and afterwards keep heading down to the Keys, which takes four hours. Navigate by following US Route 1, which at one point becomes an almost continuous span called the Seven Mile Bridge. Moor up outside boutique hotel Casa Morada (T 305 664 0044) on Islamorada. Key West lies at the tip and feels like the end of the world. It remains charmingly unspoiled, with houses covered in creepers and bougainvillea.

NSU Art Museum, Fort Lauderdale

Designed by Edward Larrabee Barnes and opened in 1986, NSU anchors a burgeoning arts hub on the New River. Highlights are an extensive collection of William J Glackens' realist paintings, sculptures by local talent Teresita Fernández and an installation by Miami-based Haitian Edouard Duval-Carrié. Nearby, FAT Village (T 954 760 5900) is the city's answer to Wynwood, boasting street murals and native works showcased inside vast warehouses. Creative types gather at JB&C (T 954 368 2718) and in the garden at eccentric cocktail lounge The Wilder (T 954 683 9453), while a glittery crowd heads to oceanfront eateries such as Dune (T 754 900 4059). Brightline runs a regular train service from Downtown Miami to Fort Lauderdale (it takes 30 minutes).
1 E Las Olas Boulevard, T 954 525 5500, www.nsuartmuseum.org

Sarasota

It's hard to believe this small community, 370km from Miami, is home to some of the finest midcentury architecture in the US. The Sarasota School was inspired by Bauhaus and the postwar exigencies that prompted the creation of the Case Study Houses in California. Features included the use of new industrial materials such as cast concrete beams, open floor plans and overhanging roofs that caught the breeze and helped reduce the heat. Paul Rudolph, Victor Lundy, Tim Siebert and Gene Leedy have all left their mark here. Fine examples of the style include Lundy's 1959 St Paul's Lutheran Church (above), Rudolph's restored 1954 cabañas at the Sanderling Beach Club and his ground-breaking 1953 Umbrella House (opposite); book tours via the foundation's website. *www.sarasotaarchitecturalfoundation.org*

NOTES
SKETCHES AND MEMOS

RESOURCES
CITY GUIDE DIRECTORY

A

Adrienne Arsht Center for the Performing Arts 009
1300 Biscayne Boulevard
T 305 949 6722
www.arshtcenter.org

Agua Spa 029
Delano
1685 Collins Avenue
T 305 674 6100
www.delano-hotel.com

Alchemist 094
Level 5
1111 Lincoln Road
T 305 531 4815
www.shopalchemist.com

Alter 042
223 NW 23rd Street
T 305 573 5996
www.altermiami.com

Amara at Paraiso 044
3101 NE 7th Avenue
T 305 702 5528
www.amaraatparaiso.com

American Airlines Arena 080
601 Biscayne Boulevard
T 786 777 1000
www.aaarena.com

The Anderson 031
709 NE 79th Street
T 305 757 3368
www.theandersonmiami.com

Arango 064
5864 Sunset Drive
T 305 661 4229
www.arango-design.com

Art Nouveau Gallery 071
348 NW 29th Street
T 305 573 4661
www.artnouveau-gallery.com

ArtCenter/South Florida 064
924 Lincoln Road
T 305 674 8278
www.artcentersf.org

Atlantis 014
2025 Brickell Avenue

B

Bacardi Complex 086
2100 Biscayne Boulevard
T 305 377 1140
www.youngarts.org

Bal Harbour Shops 088
9700 Collins Avenue
T 305 866 0311
www.balharbourshops.com

Base Superstore 089
2215 NW 2nd Avenue
T 305 531 4982
www.baseworld.com

The Bass 036
2100 Collins Avenue
T 305 673 7530
www.thebass.org

Biscayne Plaza Shopping Center 081
NE 79th Street

Blue Collar 053
6730 Biscayne Boulevard
T 305 756 0366
www.bluecollarmiami.com

HOTELS
ADDRESSES AND ROOM RATES

The Betsy 028
Room rates:
double, from $400;
Skyline Penthouse, from $2,600
1440 Ocean Drive
T 305 531 6100
www.thebetsyhotel.com

Casa Morada 100
Room rates:
double, from $500
136 Madeira Road
Islamorada
Florida Keys
T 305 664 0044
www.casamorada.com

Casa Tua 051
Room rates:
Suite, from $460
1700 James Avenue
T 305 673 0973
www.casatualifestyle.com

COMO Metropolitan 020
Room rates:
double, from $370;
Ocean View Suite, from $830
2445 Collins Avenue
T 305 695 3600
www.comohotels.com

The Confidante 016
Room rates:
double, from $190
4041 Collins Avenue
T 305 424 1234
www.hyatt.com

Delano 029
Room rates:
double, from $560
1685 Collins Avenue
T 305 672 2000
www.delano-hotel.com

East 025
Room rates:
double, from $350;
Corner King, from $480;
East Suite, from $3,380
788 Brickell Plaza
T 305 712 7000
www.east-miami.com

Edition 021
Room rates:
double, from $530
2901 Collins Avenue
T 786 257 4500
www.editionhotels.com/miami-beach

Faena 018
Room rates:
double, from $950;
Premier Oceanfront Corner Suite,
from $1,300
3201 Collins Avenue
T 305 534 8800
www.faena.com/miami-beach

Fontainebleau 081
Room rates:
double, from $400
4441 Collins Avenue
T 800 548 8886
www.fontainebleau.com

Four Seasons 016
Room rates:
double, from $360
1435 Brickell Avenue
T 305 358 3535
www.fourseasons.com

Four Seasons at The Surf Club 022
Room rates:
double, from $1,200;
Cabana Studio and Marybelle
Penthouse Suite, prices on request
9011 Collins Avenue
T 305 381 3333
www.fourseasons.com/surfside

Freehand 016
Room rates:
double, from $110
2727 Indian Creek Drive
T 305 531 2727
www.thefreehand.com

The Island House 097
Room rates:
double, from $400
Mahogany Hill Western Road
Nassau
The Bahamas
T 242 698 6300
www.the-island-house.com

Kimpton Epic 016
Room rates:
double, from $260
270 Biscayne Boulevard
T 305 424 5226
www.epichotel.com

Kimpton Surfcomber 016
Room rates:
double, from $110
1717 Collins Avenue
T 305 532 7715
www.surfcomber.com

Mandarin Oriental 016
Room rates:
double, from $300
500 Brickell Key Drive
T 305 913 8288
www.mandarinoriental.com

Mondrian 057
Room rates:
double, from $200
1100 West Avenue
T 305 514 1500
www.morganshotelgroup.com

Mr C 016
Room rates:
double, from $230
2988 McFarlane Road
T 866 786 4173
www.mrccoconutgrove.com

Nautilus by Arlo 024
Room rates:
double, from $360
1825 Collins Avenue
T 305 503 5700
www.arlohotels.com/nautilus-by-arlo

New Yorker 080
Room rates:
double, from $90
6500 Biscayne Boulevard
T 305 759 5823
www.newyorkerboutiquehotel.us

1 Hotel 016
Room rates:
double, from $330
2341 Collins Avenue
T 305 604 1000
www.1hotels.com

The Plymouth 016
Room rates:
double, from $160
336 21st Street
T 305 602 5000
www.theplymouth.com

Soho Beach House 017
Room rates:
double, from $270;
Beachside room, from $480
4385 Collins Avenue
T 786 507 7900
www.sohobeachhouse.com

The Standard 035
Room rates:
double, from $250
40 Island Avenue
T 305 673 1717
www.standardhotels.com

The Vagabond Hotel 030
Room rates:
double, from $160
7301 Biscayne Boulevard
T 305 400 8420
www.thevagabondhotelmiami.com

W Fort Lauderdale 096
Room rates:
double, from $290
401 N Fort Lauderdale Beach Boulevard
Fort Lauderdale
T 954 414 8200
www.marriott.com

W Miami 013
Room rates:
double, from $440
485 Brickell Avenue
T 305 503 4400
www.marriott.com

W South Beach 026
Room rates:
double, from $500;
Extreme Wow suite, from $17,000
2201 Collins Avenue
T 305 938 3000
www.wsouthbeach.com

WALLPAPER* CITY GUIDES

Executive Editor
Jeremy Case

Author
Rainbow Nelson

Photography Editor
Rebecca Moldenhauer

Art Editor
Jade R Arroyo

Senior Sub-Editor
Sean McGeady

Editorial Assistant
Josh Lee

Contributors
Linda Lee
Belle Place
Olivia Berry
Katarzyna Puchowska
George Greenhill
Tom and Victoria Drechsler
Erin Newberg
Pablo de Ritis
Rene González
Avra Jain

Interns
Chihting Chao
Niina Lopes
Alex Merola

Miami Imprint
First published 2007
Fifth edition 2019

ISBN 978 0 7148 7825 6

More City Guides
www.phaidon.com/travel

Follow us
@wallpaperguides

Contact
wcg@phaidon.com

Original Design
Loran Stosskopf

Map Illustrator
Russell Bell

Production Controller
Gif Jittiwutikarn

**Assistant Production
Controller**
Lily Rodgers

Wallpaper* Magazine
161 Marsh Wall
London E14 9AP
contact@wallpaper.com

Wallpaper*® is a
registered trademark
of TI Media

Phaidon Press Limited
Regent's Wharf
All Saints Street
London N1 9PA

Phaidon Press Inc
65 Bleecker Street
New York, NY 10012

All prices and venue
information are correct
at time of going to press,
but are subject to change.

A CIP Catalogue record for
this book is available from
the British Library.

PHOTOGRAPHERS

Lisa Petrole
Portofino Tower, p012
Faena, pp018-019
Como Metropolitan, p020
Four Seasons at The Surf
Club, p022, p023
The Nautilus, p024
East, p025
The Betsy, p028
The Bass, p037
Stubborn Seed, p039
Planta South Beach, p041
Alter, p042
Sherwoods, p043
Amara at Paralso, p044,
p045
Upland, p046
Plant, p047
Chotto Matte, pp048-049
Casa Tua, p050, p051
Three at Wynwood Arcade,
p052
Bodega Taqueria y Tequila,
pp054-55
Sweet Liberty, p056
Kyu, p058, p059
Juvia, p060
Karla Ferguson, p063
Museum Garage,
pp068-069
ICA, p075
Wynwood Walls, p079
MiMo architecture, p081
Bacardi Complex,
p086, p087

Base Superstore, p089
TenOverSix, p090
The Webster, p091
Fabrice Tardieu, p095

Robin Hill
1111 Lincoln Road,
pp010-011
Edition, p021
The Vagabond Hotel,
p030, p031
PAMM, p034
Mignonette, p053
Hyde Beach, p057
MC Kitchen, p061
John Henry sculpture,
p065
Art Nouveau Gallery, p071
United States Post Office,
p083
Miami Marine Stadium,
pp084-085
Florida Southern College,
pp098-099

Zachary Balber
Fredric Snitzer Gallery,
pp072-073
The Bass, p036

Steven Brooke
NSU Art Museum, p101

David Burk
Soho Beach House, p017

Mike Butler
W South Beach, p027

Rene Gonzalez
Stiltsville, p100

Stephan Göttlicher
Luis Pons dresser, p070

Ken Hyden
Small Tea, pp092-093

Thomas Loof
Sarasota, p103

Fredrik Nilsen
ICA, p074

Paul Rudolph
Sarasota, p102

Michael Stavaridis
Glass Tower, p082
Alchemist, p094

Claudia Uribe Touri
Miami city view,
inside front cover
Icon Brickell, p013
Atlantis Condominium,
pp014-015
New World Centre, p038

MIAMI

A COLOUR-CODED GUIDE TO THE HOT 'HOODS

CORAL GABLES/COCONUT GROVE
Come here for the Mediterranean-style buildings, chichi boutiques and pretty waterfront

SOUTH BEACH
World-class contemporary architecture has joined the art deco hotels and party scene

MIMO DISTRICT
The rejuvenation of Biscayne Boulevard has begun as its 1950s MiMo motels are reborn

DESIGN DISTRICT
A concentration of fashion brands, sprawling interiors showrooms and flash restaurants

DOWNTOWN/WYNWOOD
While the financial centre sprouts new towers, Wynwood attracts hip bars and galleries

MIAMI BEACH
Revamps of classic hotels and the arrival of The Surf Club have revitalised this stretch

For a full description of each neighbourhood, see the Introduction.
Featured venues are colour-coded, according to the district in which they are located.